GYMNASTICS FUN & GAMES

Patty Hacker, Phd
South Dakota State University

Eric Malmberg, EdD
State University of New York, Cortland

Jim Nance, EdS
University of Kentucky

Human Kinetics

Library of Congress Cataloging-in-Publication Data

Hacker, Patty, 1951-
    Gymnastics fun and games / Patty Hacker, Eric Malmberg, Jim Nance.
      p. cm.
    Includes bibliographical references (p.   ).
    ISBN 0-88011-557-2
    1. Gymnastics--Study and teaching. 2. Games. I. Malmberg, Eric,
  1952-   . II. Nance, Jim, 1938-   . III. Title.
  GV461.H23   1996   96-15781
  796.41'07--dc20   CIP

ISBN: 0-88011-557-2

Acquisitions Editor: Scott Wikgren; **Developmental Editor:** Kristine Enderle; **Assistant Editors:** Julie Marx Ohnemus and Sandra Merz Bott; **Editorial Assistant:** Coree Schutter; **Copyeditor:** Karen Bojda; **Proofreader:** Dawn Barker; **Graphic Artists:** Angie Snyder, Kathy Fuoss, Yvonne Winsor, and Ruby Zimmerman; **Graphic Designer:** Robert Reuther; **Cover Designer:** Jack Davis; **Photographer (cover):** Will Zehr; **Illustrators:** Tim Stiles and Jennifer Delmotte; **Printer:** United Graphics

Human Kinetics books are available at special discounts for bulk purchase. Special editions or book excerpts can also be created to specification. For details, contact the Special Sales Manager at Human Kinetics.

Printed in the United States of America   10 9 8 7 6 5

Human Kinetics
Web site: www.HumanKinetics.com

United States: Human Kinetics, P.O. Box 5076, Champaign, IL 61825-5076
800-747-4457
e-mail: humank@hkusa.com

Canada: Human Kinetics, 475 Devonshire Road, Unit 100, Windsor, ON N8Y 2L5
800-465-7301 (in Canada only)
e-mail: orders@hkcanada.com

Europe: Human Kinetics, 107 Bradford Road, Stanningley
Leeds LS28 6AT, United Kingdom
+44 (0) 113 255 5665
e-mail: hk@hkeurope.com

Australia: Human Kinetics, 57A Price Avenue, Lower Mitcham, South Australia 5062
08 8277 1555
e-mail: liaw@hkaustralia.com

New Zealand: Human Kinetics, Division of Sports Distributors NZ Ltd.
P.O. Box 300 226 Albany, North Shore City, Auckland
0064 9 448 1207
e-mail: blairc@hknewz.com

Contents

Game Finder

Name	Game No.	Type	Skills	Grade	Level	Page No.
Add-On	39	S	r, b, f, g	2 - 6	L	89
Alphabet Soup	23	S	b, g, l	2 - 5	L - M	58
Balance Builders	18	S	b	K - 6	L	48
Balance Puzzles	22	S	b, g	K - 2	L	56
Balance Tag	28	S	b, l	K - 4	L	68
Balloon Relay Race	34	S	g, r	K - 4	L - M	80
Banana Split	49	CE	s	2 - 6	L - M	110
Barracuda Barricade	29	S	g, l	K - 4	L	70
Building Bridges	8	W	g, l, f	2 - 6	L	26
Card Shark Fitness	14	S	f, g, b, r	3 - 8	L - M	40
Cover Tag	2	W	l, g	K - 3	L	16
Cross the Alligator Pit	44	CE	f, s	2 - 8	L - H	100
Cupcake Walk	36	S	g	2 - 6	M	84
Footsie Rolls	25	S	r	2 - 6	L	62
Four Corners, Four Poses	32	S	b	2 - 6	M	76
Giant's Treasure	16	S	b	K - 3	L	44
Gymnastics Board Game	46	CE	f, s	3 - 8	L	104
Gymnastics Obstacle Course	6	W	g	K - 2	L	22
Gymnastics Trivia	13	W	—	K - 8	L	36

Contributors

The following people contributed ideas or activities that we used in developing this book.

Dave Adlard
Pittsburg, CA

Tammy Aronson
North Myrtle Beach Gymnastics
North Myrtle Beach, NC

Karen Bucaro
Plano, TX

Rich Fabris
Leonia, NJ

Susan Floyd
Augusta, GA

Marci Germani
El Centro, CA

Patty Hacker
South Dakota State University
Brookings, SD

Mike Henty
Fingerlakes Gym Center
Auburn, NY

Louise Janecky
Los Alamos, NM

Margie Kelly
Savannah, GA

Claire Kew
Chagrin Falls, OH

Eric Malmberg
State University of New York
Cortland, NY

Melanie Moore
Gold Medal Gymnastics
Brookings, SD

Pat Murphy
Moultrie YMCA
Moultrie, GA

Jan Nance
Stamping Ground, KY

Jim Nance
University of Kentucky—Lexington
Lexington, KY

Rae Pica
Center Barnstead, NH

Stephen Posner
Springfield College
Springfield, MA

Prineville Gymnastics
Prineville, OR

Lisa Shuck
Bulleen, Victoria
Australia

Harry Tate
San Mateo Gymnastics Center
Belmont, CA

Peter Werner
University of South Carolina
Columbia, SC

Preface

The teaching of gymnastics has enjoyed a long history within the field of physical education. Over time many different forms of gymnastics have emerged to become the center of curricular focus. Jahn's gymnastics, Swedish gymnastics and military gymnastics, medical gymnastics, and competitive Olympic gymnastics are all models that have at one time or another dominated the field.

Currently, the teaching of gymnastics games and activities in public schools again appears to be undergoing a period of transition. Emphasis is changing from competitive or sport models of teaching gymnastics to a more developmentally appropriate model that focuses on body conditioning, strength and endurance, flexibility, and skill development. This curricular transition has left many educators asking practical questions such as "What kinds of gymnastics games can I offer to supplement my tumbling or gymnastics unit?" "Are there games and activities I can use that are 'school appropriate' in terms of safety and time efficiency?" "I have so little background in gymnastics; I know only Olympic or competitive gymnastics. Where can I get some ideas? I want gymnastics to be fun for my students." The materials in this book attempt to address these concerns.

This book is a compilation of games and activities to supplement teaching gymnastics in an educational setting. These games and activities are intended to develop creativity, spatial awareness, coordination, strength, and agility. Unlike competitive gymnastics, this book has no stunts, routines, or choreographed exercises. Instead it offers games and activities to help physical education teachers enhance the learning of gymnastics skills in an interesting, challenging, noncompetitive, and fun atmosphere. All these games and activities have been field-tested in educational settings across the United States, in public schools as well as in private recreational programs, YMCAs, and clubs. We offer them to you to use, adapt, modify, and make your own.

Acknowledgments

Many thanks go to the teachers in both public schools and private programs who shared their ideas with us. They provided a good springboard for the material in this book. Thanks also goes to the Department of Safety and Education of USA Gymnastics for the support they gave in soliciting ideas from the gymnastics community and public school teachers, as well as for providing us with an opportunity to get together for very intensive work sessions while we brainstormed, debated, wrote, and rewrote the material in this book.

Credits

Safety responsibilities adapted, by permission, from USA Gymnastics, 1994, *USA Gymnastics Safety Handbook* (Indianapolis, IN: USA Gymnastics),56.

Figures on pp. 9-11. Reprinted, by permission, from American Coaching Effectiveness Program, 1992, *Rookie Coaches Gymnastics Guide* (Champaign, IL: Human Kinetics Publishers), 55-57.

Warm-Up Activities table, p. 8. Reprinted, by permission, from American Coaching Effectiveness Program, 1992, *Rookie Coaches Gymnastics Guide* (Champaign, IL: Human Kinetics Publishers), 55.

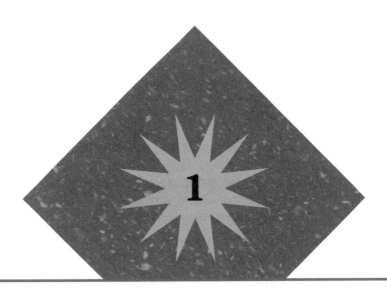

Introduction

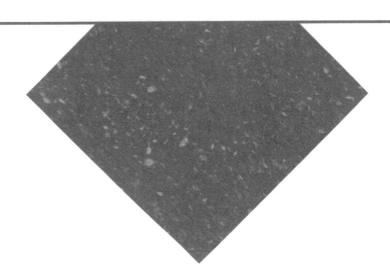

number where the game can be found. The skill components are indicated by lower-case letters: *l* for locomotor, *r* for rolls, *b* for balance, *f* for flexibility, *g* for gymnastics or tumbling skill, *s* for strength. For example, the game finder key for the game Movement Puzzle is type S (skill development); skills b, g, l (balance, gymnastics, locomotor); grade K-8; and level L-H (low to high complexity).

Using the Glossary and Other Supplemental Materials

The glossary defines terms that are specific to gymnastics skills as we use them. All terms are listed alphabetically and are defined using language that does not assume familiarity with gymnastics terminology. The reading list shows other books with good activities that are useful resources for your work in tumbling and gymnastics activities. We have also included a sample equipment checklist that can help you maintain a safe environment for gymnastics. Many of our ideas for games come from other teachers, so on pages 120-121 is a form that you may use to send us activity ideas that you'd like to share with other teachers. It is always a challenge to try to meet the needs of an audience one hasn't met, so if using any of these games brings something to mind that you would like to share, please send it along.

Safety Responsibilities for Teachers

Safety is always a primary concern when teaching and supervising gymnastics and tumbling activities. In a very real sense, the safety of students is the first obligation of the teacher.

The teacher should understand the importance of general safety awareness by all those involved in gymnastics activities. Participants include not just the students, but also the teachers, parents, and other supervisors. In short, safety is everyone's responsibility.

As a teacher of gymnastics activities, you should be aware of your specific contractual or professional obligations for the safety and well-being of your students. It is all too easy to forget what common sense tells us about selecting activities for our students, particularly when they are clamoring to do "fun things." In gymnastics and tumbling, as in all activities, your experience and good sense should dictate which activities are selected for class. All teachers of any physical activity must always know and keep in mind their specific duties and responsibilities to the students. More information about gymnastics safety can be found in two sources, *The Rookie Coaches Gymnastics Guide* from Human Kinetics and *The USA Gymnastics Safety Handbook* (3rd edition) from USA Gymnastics.

In general, your responsibilities and duties include the following:

Fulfill mission statement, goals, and objectives. Every school, whether public or private, has a mission statement that defines its purpose for existence. Goals and objectives are developed that flow logically from the mission statement. All activities you teach should be planned to help meet these goals and objectives and ultimately fulfill the school's mission.

Plan the activity properly. You need to develop clear, written guidelines for class and student conduct. This includes detailed lesson plans that spell out how class should be conducted, leaving no room for misunderstanding should someone else have to teach the class.

Provide proper instruction. Recognize and understand necessary sequences and progressions for teaching gymnastics and tumbling skills. There are many good texts available that can help you learn these progressions if you are not familiar with them (check out the reading list on page 117). Be sure to take the time to understand the progressions!

Supervise the activity closely. This includes general or specific supervision, depending on the student, situation, and activity. The more complex the activity, the more closely the activity must be supervised. Since proper supervision is one of the biggest problems in a gymnasium setting, you need to clearly and immediately establish guidelines for supervision of the class.

Know your students. You should have an understanding of the general background of your students, including their limitations. In matching students for balance and other activities, make sure you consider age, height, maturity, skill level, and experience. You should also be aware of the effect of peer pressure on individual performance and plan your activities accordingly.

At some point in your lesson planning, you may need to consider modifying or adapting these activities so that students with special needs can participate safely. Children with visual impairments can work with a partner who can cue them verbally with descriptions of the tasks to be performed. For children with hearing impairments, have pictures or diagrams available for them to use as a guide, or have another student demonstrate the tasks. Students who are in wheelchairs or otherwise restricted in their movement can perform those parts of the tasks that do not require assistance, or they can work with a partner who can help them through the tasks. Other children with special needs—those who are recovering from illness or have restrictions on movement due to injury—can also participate when the tasks are modified so that the movements required are more restricted and the students participate only to the extent of their abilities. For very aerobically intense activities, students can participate at a lower energy level.

Always remember to address both visual and auditory needs of all students, and prepare lessons with all students in mind.

Keep informed. You have a responsibility as a professional to regularly update your knowledge concerning proper techniques and progressions for skills in gymnastics and to keep yourself informed of new developments in teaching methods and how you can apply them to teaching gymnastics activities.

Provide a safe physical environment, including adequate and proper equipment. Facilities must be safe for those involved in the activity. Existing safety codes and standards for equipment should be met, and all equipment should be regularly maintained. Inspect your equipment periodically and repair it when necessary (keep a record of the dates of these inspections and repairs). A sample checklist is included on pages 118-119 that you can use as a guide for checking your own equipment.

Warn of inherent risks. You need to be familiar with the ordinary risks of participating in tumbling and gymnastics activities and of using equipment specific to these activities. Risks that are integral to the activities must be explained to the students in words that are appropriate for their age and comprehension levels and that they can clearly understand. As difficult as it may seem, you need to very carefully and clearly explain to your students that if they are careless in participating in gymnastics activities, they or someone else could be very seriously injured, and the injury could result in death. The goal is to learn to perform all the skills safely.

Provide appropriate emergency assistance. Students must be evaluated for injury and incapacity. You need to have a knowledge of basic emergency first aid and injury management procedures such as STOP (Stop the athlete from continuing to participate, Talk to the injured athlete and ask questions, Observe the athlete's personality and injury, Prevent further injury) and RICE (Rest the injured part, Ice, Compress, Elevate) and keep up to date on them. Have a written emergency plan and make sure you work from it. Also ensure that appropriate medical assistance is available in case of an accident.

Keep adequate records. Adequate records are important and useful aids and should be kept for all students. Records should include relevant general and medical information, progress reports, and accident reports, as well as written records of risk warnings (dates given).

When these 10 responsibilities are met, gymnastics activities can be done in an environment that is safer for all involved. Always remember, safety of the participants is the first responsibility of the teacher. Fun and enjoyment are also very important, so you should plan activities that are both safe and fun.

Do We Warm Up First?

The warm-up is an essential part of any organized program of physical activity. You need to make sure your students engage in a meaningful and well-structured warm-up for gymnastics games and activities.

There are many ways to warm up a class of learners. You may prefer a very structured warm-up in which your students perform the same activities each class meeting. Or you might decide to use a warm-up routine that allows for some variety. Whatever warm-up you choose, make sure it suits your own teaching style and prepares your students for the activities that follow. A good approach to developing warm-ups is to select activities from the following three categories:

1. Aerobic activities are intended to get the students' heart rates elevated.
2. Stretching activities are intended to warm up muscles and stretch them for the activities that follow.
3. Preparation includes any activity that prepares students for the focus of your main lesson.

Design your warm-up activities after you have decided which activities or games to add to your lesson plan. The warm-up should include general aerobic activities followed by stretching exercises. Finally, you may select exercises that help prepare your students for the particular game or activity you have chosen. After the class has completed the main lesson activity, you can complete the class with a cool-down using other warm-up or stretching activities. The timetable below helps you to plan for the warm-up portion of the class time. It includes time for introducing the lesson and for aerobic and stretching exercises. Divide the warm-up activities into preparation, aerobics, and stretching activities, as outlined in the chart. Keep in mind that the total warm-up period depends on the total amount of class time you have with your students.

Warm-Up Activities				
Activity				
	30 min	**35 min**	**40 min**	**50 min**
Organization and class instruction	1 min	1 min	1 min	1 min
Aerobics: Start slow, then increase the activity/demand	3 min	5 min	6 min	9 min
Stretching activities: Begin with large muscle groups, progress to small muscle groups; include coordination skills and games	1 min	2 min	3 min	4 min
Total warm-up period	5 min	8 min	10 min	14 min

Using music or rhythms will enhance the warm-up and add fun. Select music that appeals to the students and has a strong beat (in 4/4 or 4/8 time or an occasional waltz tempo). If music is unavailable, you can count, clap, or use a rhythm instrument such as a drum. You can also encourage your students to create their own rhythms by counting out loud, clapping, using rhythm instruments, or even doing chants or raps.

Common tag games can be used as the aerobic component in a thorough warm-up, because they serve to elevate the students' heart rates. These games also can be modified to help prepare students for the gymnastics games and activities (see chapter 2 for examples). Other warm-up activities that can be used are illustrated on pages 9-11. Remember, the idea is to use activities that interest your students, are within their skill level, and still provide a warm-up within the time constraints of your program.

Side and Shoulder Stretches. Stand with one arm extended straight up, then tilt the upper body to the opposite side, reaching the hand up and across. Repeat the stretch on the other side. For the shoulder stretch, extend one arm across the chest, grasp the raised elbow with the opposite hand, and pull the elbow toward the body. Repeat the stretch on the other side.

Modified Hurdle and Hip Stretch. Sit in a 90-degree straddle and bend one leg inward, positioning the heel against the opposite thigh. Bend at the waist and lower the torso toward the straight leg and then toward the bent leg. Switch legs and repeat the stretch.

Rear Shoulder Stretch. Using a ballet bar, low parallel bar, single rail, or low horizontal bar, stand facing away from the bar. Grasp the bar with hands slightly beyond shoulder width and thumbs facing out. Slowly push the knees and hips out away from the bar. The body arches slightly (resembling a bridge). Allow the shoulders and the back to drop below the bar.

Half-Split Stretch. Lunge forward and bend the back leg to a kneeling position. Keeping chest and shoulders upright, press hips toward the floor. Repeat the stretch on the other side.

Straddle Stretch. Sit in a 90-degree or greater straddle and slowly stretch forward and to each side. Keep the head up.

Chin-to-Chest, Ear-to-Shoulder Stretch. Slowly lower the head forward, press the chin toward the chest, then raise the head. Then slowly lower the head to the side, press the ear toward the shoulder, and raise the head.

Warm-Up Games and Activities

Shark

1	2	3

2-5 Min.

Level: Low

Goal: Warm-up

Equipment: Panel mats scattered on the floor

Formation: Scattered

Description: Before the game, teacher explains the following commands and actions:

Command	Action
"Pegleg"	Hop on one foot
"Walk the plank"	Straddle stand and cover your eyes with your hands. Move knees as if entire body is shaking with fear.
"Land ahoy"	Player 1 on hands and knees. Player 2 stands with one foot on Player 1's back with hand on forehead as if scanning the horizon.
"Shark"	Players must try to avoid being tagged by the shark.

One student is designated as the "shark," who swims about in the water (the area not covered by mats). The other children are "fish" and swim back and forth on or off the matted areas. When commands are called out, all players respond with the appropriate action. On the command "shark," the fish are in danger of being eaten by the shark. The shark tries to tag the fish. The only way the fish can be safe is to lie down flat on the mat. Any of the fish tagged by the shark join the shark in tagging other fish.

Application to gymnastics: This activity can help develop quick reflexes and good muscular response, which are important for more complex gymnastics movements in floor exercise and vaulting.

–Review all skills to be performed and make sure that students understand and are able to perform them.

–Make sure all students understand the terminology used in the game—tell them the commands and ask them to explain the actions to be performed for each command.

–Have pictures to illustrate each of the skills.

–Be sure to designate a clear area for this game.

–Make sure mats are available for use as safe areas for fish.

Remind students that they are to move from one skill to the next quickly but safely. The idea is to complete the task, not necessarily to be the first one done.

Substitute a static gymnastics skill for a "safe" position. For example, students can do handstands, headstands, scales, and poses.

Cover Tag

K	1	2	3	

 2-5 Min.

Level: Low

Goal: Warm-up

Equipment: None

Formation: Scattered

Description: Common tag rules apply—that is, "it" tries to tag others who then become "it"—except the new "it" must cover the spot where tagged on his or her body with one hand.

Application to gymnastics: This activity can be used to practice gymnastics locomotor skills such as leaps, chassés, etc.

 Use tasks that will challenge but not frustrate students, such as having them touch the spot with the opposite hand or with both hands.

 –Be sure to designate a clear area for this game.

–Reinforce the concepts of general and personal space to help avoid accidents.

 This is a very short activity—do not spend a lot of time with it.

 Have students perform gymnastics locomotor movements (such as leaps, jumps, chassés, etc.) as they move around the floor.

3

Stuck in the Mud

K	1	2	3	

 2-5 Min.

Level: Low

Goal: Warm-up

Equipment: None

Formation: Scattered

Description: On the word "go," everyone except the person who is "it" takes off running. After a few seconds, "it" may move and try to tag the others. If they are tagged, they must freeze, put their hands on their heads, spread their legs (straddle stand), and call for help. They may be freed and return to the game when someone crawls between their legs.

Application to gymnastics: This activity can be used as a general conditioning warm-up that helps to develop endurance for later floor exercise routines and vaulting. It can also be used to practice gymnastics locomotor skills such as leaps, chassés, etc.

–Make sure the skills to be performed are selected appropriately for the performance level of the students.
–Use tasks that will challenge but not frustrate the students.

Be sure to designate a clear area for this game.

Students need to be careful when crawling under each others' legs so no one gets hurt.

–Have students freeze in a static gymnastics position, such as a scale, split, or pike-straddle stand.
–Have students perform a designated skill on being freed, such as a cartwheel or jump.

4

Thread the Needle

K	1	2	3	

 2-5 Min.

Level: Low

Goal: Warm-up

Equipment: None

Formation: Scattered

Description: Class runs in a single line following a leader, who runs in circles and spirals while performing a particular gymnastics locomotor skill such as a cat leap or chassé. The leader should move quickly and cause the line to cross itself by leading the line between following students, as if threading a needle.

Application to gymnastics: This particular activity can focus students' attention on performing different gymnastics locomotor movements. It can also help reinforce concepts of personal and general space as the students move quickly between each other.

–Reinforce performance points; that is, review all the skills to be performed to be sure that all students understand and can perform them.

–Make sure the skills selected are based on the performance level of the students. Assess student performance based on the key parts of each skill performed.

 –Be sure to monitor leader's activities.

–Remind students not to follow too closely and to watch when the leader is "threading the needle."

 Complete the task appropriately, not quickly!

 –Try balancing beanbags while following the leader.

–Focus on fundamental motor skills for the youngest children, such as running, skipping, and jumping, and on more complex skills for older children, such as leaps, gymnastics jumps, or skipping backward.

5

Push and Run

| | 2 | 3 | 4 | 5 | 6 | 7 | 8 |

 2-5 Min.

Level: Low

Goal: Warm-up

Equipment: Panel mats arranged in a large square as needed based on skill level of students

Formation: Scattered pairs

Description: Partners stand and face each other, palm to palm. One partner runs hard in place while leaning against the other student, who acts as a "wall" by providing support. Students should focus on good running form and technique, including (1) keeping feet and knees pointing straight forward, (2) lifting knees high, (3) running on the balls of the feet, and (4) extending legs fully.

Application to gymnastics: This activity reinforces proper running form, which is very important for successful vaulting and tumbling.

Remind students of important performance cues: They should not lean forward, and their bodies should be kept straight, not bent at the hips as they press into the "wall."

 –Remind students who are providing support not to collapse the "wall" while their partner is leaning into it.

–Use mats as needed based on the skill level of the students.

–Instruct the students not to step on their partner.

Gymnastics Obstacle Course

| K | 1 | 2 |

 10 Min.

Level: Low

Goal: To familiarize students with various pieces of gymnastics equipment in a nonthreatening manner

Equipment: Floor beam, panel mats, foam blocks, wedge mat

Formation: Single file at the start of the course, then scattered as students progress through the course

Description: The instructor sets up an obstacle course (see diagram), and students perform the suggested activities at each station.

Station	Activity
1	Walk, leap, or roll down the beam (carpeted if possible).
2	At end of beam, step off and jump over block (stack of mats).
3	Leapfrog over foam blocks.
4	Run, crawl, or roll up the wedge mat.
5	Jump off end of wedge mat, perform five tuck jumps on the X (marked on the floor with tape).
6	Follow the crazy maze (zigzag line on floor) using a gymnastics locomotor skill, such as chassés.
7	Perform a bridge over a beam or have students go underneath the bridge (a mat spread across two objects that will provide a space underneath for children to crawl or slither under).
8	Start over.

Application to gymnastics: Students work with gymnastics equipment and begin to practice basic gymnastics motor skills.

 –Make sure students are familiar with each of the activities in the obstacle course. Be creative with the available equipment, but keep the manufacturer's recommendations in mind at all times.

–In place of a beam for station 1, substitute mats on the floor that have a line taped on them (or two side-by-side lines about four to six inches apart).

–Use this activity as an introductory activity for the daily lesson.

–Allow students to be creative in how they move over the blocks or under the mats.

–If students cannot perform a skill the first time, let them attempt it one more time before moving on to the next station.

 –Make sure all students recognize how each piece of equipment is to be used and understand how to go safely through the obstacle course.

–Stagger each student's start through the course so that students do not run into each other.

–Set up the course so that it will challenge the students, not frustrate them.

–When students have mastered the course, do not have them go through the course again just to take up class time.

–Vary the way that sutdents go down the beam (backward, sideways, etc.).

–Have students jump up onto the high end of the wedge mat and perform rolls down (forward, log, backward, or doggy rolls).

Zipper Tag

| | 3 | 4 | 5 | 6 | |

5-7 Min.

Level: Low

Goal: Warm-up

Equipment: None (or matted area)

Formation: Scattered

Description: Before this mass tag game begins, students form teams of three. On the "go" signal, all students scatter and try to "unzip" other students not on their team. Unzipping is done by running a finger lightly down another player's back while he or she is not looking. Unzipped players must sit where they were caught until a teammate "zips them up" by running a finger lightly up their backs.

Application to gymnastics: This activity can be used to practice gymnastics locomotor skills such as leaps, chassés, etc.

 When using gymnastics locomotor skills, have students orally review the performance cues for each skill to be utilized.

 Be sure to designate a clear area for this game.

 –Remind students about general and personal space and how to avoid accidents.

–This activity is used as a general warm-up—it is not the focus of the entire lesson.

–Once students are downed, they must remember not to move until they have been "zipped up."

 Use gymnastics locomotor skills (e.g. chassé, assemblé, leap) to move around the playing area.

Building Bridges

8

| 2 | 3 | 4 | 5 | 6 |

10 Min.

Level: Low

Goal: Warm-up

Equipment: Panel mats

Formation: Pairs

Description: Students form pairs and perform the following activities:

Activity	Description
Under and over	In pairs, one student makes a bridge and the partner crawls under.
Cross bridges	One partner makes a bridge by arching backward, and the other makes a bridge by arching forward over the top. Then the students switch positions.
Pirouette bridge	Start on all fours (on hands and feet, stomach down toward the floor). Roll sideways through to a bridge position without moving forward or backward. Repeat in the other direction.

Application to gymnastics: Practicing bridge positions improves back flexibility and shoulder and arm strength. Key performance points include keeping shoulders over hands, eyes looking back at fingertips (head back), feet and hands flat on the floor, and back arched.

Under and over   Cross bridges

Pirouette bridge

 –Reinforce performance points for the skill. Have students say the key parts of the bridge before they actually perform the skill.

–Students will need to make a bridge and stretch the relevant muscles and joints before doing this activity. Have pictures to show the correct performance of the skill, or demonstrate the skill with a partner.

–Set up criteria for successful completion of the task using the key performance points for assessing the students.

 –Be sure that students do not lift their hands or feet up off the floor (except when turning over) so that bridges will not collapse on each other.

–This activity should be performed only on a matted surface.

 Remind students of key performance points: "Look at your hands while performing the bridge. Try to keep arms extended while in the bridge position. Keep feet flat on the floor. Try to keep your shoulders over your hands."

 Have students develop their own bridge creations.

9

Human Circles

 10 Min.

Level: Medium

Goal: An understanding of how different body parts can create circular motion

Equipment: Floor exercise or wrestling mat, if available, or panel mats arranged in a large square

Formation: Circles scattered around matted area

Description: Students hold hands and form a large circle. The large circle then divides into two circles, then four, and so on, until circles consist of pairs and groups of three. Individual students then try to create circles using various body parts, such as hands, arms, legs, and feet. Next the students use body parts to perform skills that use circling movements, such as rolls, cartwheels, hip circles, and so on.

Application to gymnastics: Students warm up various parts of their bodies by working on circular motions. Circular motions help develop range of motion in joints that are involved in more advanced skills in tumbling and working on uneven bars. These skills include walkovers, handsprings, and swinging or circling skills.

Talk with students about parts of their bodies that can make circles. Students can demonstrate these circles.

 If students will be performing rolls, make sure they work on a matted surface.

 When working with partners, students should be paired with partners of comparable skill level.

 —Circles can be made while sitting, lying down, doing shoulder stands, and so on.

—Students can make other shapes, such as triangles, squares, and so on.

10

Knee Touch Tag

		4	5	6	7	8

 10 Min.

Level: Low

Goal: General warm-up to reinforce gymnastics skills

Equipment: None

Formation: Scattered

Description: In this tag game, all players try to tag other players' knees. Tagged players must do three gymnastics skills designated by the teacher (e.g., rolls, leaps, cartwheels). Players may not cover their knees with their hands to avoid being tagged.

Review all skills to be performed to be sure that students understand and are able to perform them.

 –Students must pay close attention to where they move when trying to avoid others.

–Students need to remember to touch, not slap, other players' knees.

 This is a short tag game—don't play too long!

 Students have a safe zone to go to when completing tasks.

Snake

| | 2 | 3 | 4 | 5 | 6 | |

 10 Min.

Level: Low

Goal: Warm-up

Equipment: Mats

Formation: Pairs

Description: The students lie down in pairs on their stomachs, one in front of the other, head to foot. The person in back grasps the feet of the person in front. The two students begin to slither across the mat and attach themselves to another pair. All pairs attach to make one long "snake." Once attached, the snake tries to move about.

Application to gymnastics: This activity is used for general warm-up prior to the main lesson focus activity. It should be used to help students learn and practice body control, coordination, and tightness.

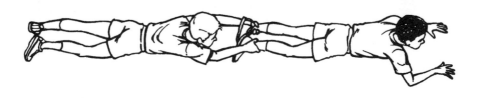

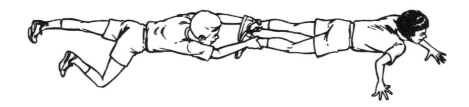

Designate a method of pairing up (alphabetically, by height, birthday, skill level, etc.) prior to explaining the activity to the students.

 –Use proper matting.
–Students are not to kick their legs.

 –This cooperative activity is not a race, and students should be patient and work as a group.
–Remind students to stay connected.

 The completed snake assumes designated formations, such as a circle, coil, knot, or rolling over.

Partner Grapevine

 5 Min.

Level: Low

Goal: To develop flexibility

Equipment: None

Formation: Pairs

Description: The students form pairs and work in a personal space. Partners hold hands and stretch by stepping over each others' arms, turning, and so on, without letting go of each others' hands.

Application to gymnastics: This activity improves students' flexibility, which is important for many gymnastics movements.

34

–Make sure partners are matched according to size and ability level.

–At least one foot of each partner should remain on the floor throughout movement.

 –Remind students to proceed slowly so no one gets stretched too far.

–No flipping!

 Remind students not to release hands—this is what makes the activity challenging and fun!

 Use groups of three to five (but no more than five) students.

Gymnastics Trivia

  Time varies depending on the trivia facts. This game is interspersed with regular class activity.

Level: Low

Goal: To help students learn about important people and events in the history of gymnastics at the national and international levels

Equipment: Gymnastics facts (which can be obtained from a variety of sources) written on index cards, paper, or posters

Description: The instructor can teach trivia throughout the class period. Find pieces of information that complement the focus activity for the day, and teach the information to students in class. Trivia instruction can be in the form of an informal quiz or simply telling students the information, showing them the information, or displaying it in the classroom or gymnasium in writing and pictures. Examples of trivia include the following facts:

- In 1952 the uneven bars were the newest Olympic event.
- The Romanian gymnast Nadia Comaneci captured perfect scores in the 1976 Olympics.
- Cathy Rigby was injured prior to the 1972 Olympic trials, but because of her importance to the U.S. team, the United States Olympic Committee (USOC) allowed her to join the team.
- Gymnastics etiquette includes not chewing gum and not wearing jewelry while in uniform and saluting the judges prior to and after performing each routine.
- The U.S. gymnastics team did not compete in the 1980 Olympics because the United States boycotted the games that year. (The 1980 Olympics were held in Moscow—another trivia fact.)
- The 1984 Olympic gold medal was won by the U.S. men's gymnastics team.
- Kurt Thomas invented the Thomas Flair in 1976.
- In the 1800s the first pommel horse was made of wood and looked like a real horse with real horse hair tail and even a leather saddle!

–Intersperse these pieces of information throughout your lesson for the day, but be careful not to overemphasize the trivia.

–Make sure that the trivia is relevant to the lesson you are teaching.

–Use trivia about the rules and history of gymnastics as well as trivia about famous people.

–This activity does not have a movement component; it is used to increase students' knowledge about the sport of gymnastics. This activity works best when interspersed with movement activities.

–Gymnastics trivia should be fun—do not make it stressful for students by expecting them to memorize all the details that you give them.

–Focus the trivia on one particular gymnastics event.

–Focus the information on Special Olympic gymnastics.

–Students can bring a piece of trivia about gymnastics that they have found in the library.

–If the information is important and you want students to remember it, make a set of question cards and answer cards that students can use as study aids. For an opening activity, as students come into class, they can each select a question card and match it to the answer card they think is correct. Review of the matches can be done as a closure activity at the end of the class.

–Students can match terms or trivia to photos of skills.

Skill Development Games and Activities

Card Shark Fitness

| | 3 | 4 | 5 | 6 | 7 | 8 |

 10 Min.

Level: Low-Medium

Goal: Development of any selected gymnastics skills and exercises

Equipment: Panel mats, playing cards, four posters with playing card suit symbols, four lists or pictures of various gymnastics skills, music and equipment to play it on

Formation: Suit posters are hung on each wall (one suit per wall) with lists or pictures of skills hung beside them. In the center of the gym floor, place two decks of playing cards scattered face down. Children are scattered around the floor.

Description: When music begins, students pick up one card each from the center and then run quickly to the wall that matches the suit of the card. Beside each poster on the wall is a list of three or four different skills to be performed. Each skill must be performed the number of times indicated by the playing card (numbered cards count at face value, jacks are 11, queens are 12, kings are 13, and aces are 14). For example, if a child picks up a nine of spades, he or she quickly runs to the spade wall and does each skill indicated nine times. After completing the skills, students keep their original cards and go back to pick up another. If the new card is of the same suit, it is returned to the pile and another card is chosen of a suit not yet drawn. After students have been to each wall once, they add up their points (by adding up their cards) either in their heads or on paper. Students try to accumulate as many points as possible each time they play this game, and points are cumulative.

Application to gymnastics: This game provides students with an opportunity to practice a variety of gymnastics skills while warming up or working on fitness. Skills must be performed quickly but correctly, as they would need to be done during a gymnastics routine.

 −Make sure the skills are selected appropriately for the performance level of the students. Use tasks that will challenge but not frustrate the students.

−Review all skills to be performed to be sure that students understand and are able to perform them.

−Have pictures to illustrate each skill, or have a student demonstrate each skill as you describe it to the other students.

−Make sure all students understand the terminology, the names of the skills, how skills should look, and how to perform them.

−Reinforce key performance points for each skill.

−Assess student performance based on the key parts of the skills being performed.

−After students accumulate a predetermined number of points, let them select the skills that will be performed.

 Make sure space is adequate for all children to perform the selected skills. Reinforce the concepts of general and personal space so that students don't run into each other as they move from wall to wall.

 Remind students that they are on their honor to perform each skill the required number of times.

 −Use only two walls (for instance, red cards and black cards).
−Vary the tasks to be performed.

Jump the Sock

K   1   2   3

 10 Min.

Level: Low

Goal: To reinforce jumping skills (tuck, straddle, pike, etc.) and promote development of muscular strength

Equipment: Rope 7 to 9 feet (2 to 2.75 meters) long with a sock tied to one end (one for each group)

Formation: Circles of 8 to 10 students

Description: Divide class into groups of 8 to 10 students. Each group forms a circle standing arms' length apart, with one student in the middle holding one end of the rope. The student in the middle designates the jump to be used (e.g., tuck, straddle, or pike jump) then begins to turn in place, swinging the rope in a circle along the floor. Students use the designated jump to jump over the sock as the end of the rope passes under them. If a student misses the rope or performs an incorrect jump, he or she replaces the rope turner in the center. If there are few misses, a time limit can be set for being rope turner.

Application to gymnastics: Students learn and practice specific gymnastics jumps.

–Students can use a bean bag or sock in the toe to give more weight.

–Make groups large enough to accommodate the entire class but small enough to allow for high participation.

–Frequently rotate the rope turner in the middle.

–The teacher selects the jumps to be performed.

–When teaching the jumps, give students descriptive cues for performance, then quiz them on those cues as they or a partner performs the jumps.

–Make sure students keep the free end of the rope on or very close to the ground to avoid hitting jumpers.

–Allow rope turners to restart only when jumpers are ready.

–Stress cooperation between jumpers and the rope turner, especially if the rope gets tangled in the feet of jumpers.

–Make sure the sock is tied securely to the end of the rope.

This is a quick activity used to reinforce the learning of jumping skills.

–Add twists for more highly skilled students.

–Vary the speed of the turning rope.

–Vary the height of the turning rope (up to but no higher than the jumpers' knees).

Giant's Treasure

K	1	2	3	

20 Min.

Level: Low

Goal: To practice balances such as arabesques or pike straddles

Equipment: Beanbags

Formation: Parallel lines as in diagram

Description: Either the teacher or a selected student is the "giant." The giant stands with his or her back to the group and guards a line of beanbag treasures. The students line up across from the giant at the starting line. Their object is to retrieve the beanbag treasures from the giant and return to the starting line. While the giant's back is turned, the children must use previously designated locomotor skills, such as walking, leaping, or hopping, to approach the treasure. The giant shouts the name of a pose. Students strike that pose when the giant says "freeze." The giant then turns around to face the students. Students who wobble, lose their balance, or freeze in an incorrect pose must go back to the starting line (or back to the treasure line on the return trip).

The giant then turns around and allows the students to continue to move toward the treasure. The game continues until all the beanbag treasures have been taken back to the starting line.

Application to gymnastics: Children learn specific gymnastics balance poses and how to create these shapes after traveling.

–Before you begin, review all the balance poses and traveling skills to be performed. Make sure that students understand the terms: Do they know the name and key points for performing the skill?

–Give the children time to practice each balance pose and traveling skill.

–Change giants frequently to give more students an opportunity to name skills.

–Use the entire gymnasium to move in, particularly if there are many students.

–Allow the students to use only poses that require upright or seated balances.

Be lenient in judging wobbles or loss of balance.

–Vary the locomotor skills students use to get to the treasure.

–Have giants demonstrate the pose when they call out the name. All students must mimic the pose shown.

–The giant demonstrates rather than names a pose: The giant shouts "freeze," then turns around and strikes a pose. Students must freeze and shout out the name of the pose.

17

Rope Swing

 7 Min.

Level: Low

Goal: To reinforce jumping skills

Equipment: Jump ropes (one for every four to six students)

Formation: Lines

Description: Students form groups of four to six. Two students in the group each hold one end of a rope, swinging it back and forth. Other students in the group jump the rope as it swings back and forth, doing the jump selected by the instructor, such as a tuck, pike-straddle, or star jump.

Application to gymnastics: Students practice specific gymnastics jumping skills (tuck, pike-straddle, etc.).

–Students should take turns being the rope swingers. Every three to four jumps or when a student misses a jump, change the rope swingers. Student swingers determine the jump to perform.

–Have students say key parts of the jump skills as they perform them. Assess student performance based on the key parts of the skills.

–Make sure the swingers drop the rope if feet get tangled up in it.

–Start out with the rope at a height that allows immediate success in jumps. Perform the jumps without the rope before starting the activity.

–Review key performance points of each jump before having students perform the jumps.

–Use pictures of the jumps as well as visual and verbal cues for those students needing additional assistance.

–Set up a series of ropes to jump over, selecting a specific jump for each rope. (This variation helps with sequencing skills.) After finishing the sequence, students take the first rope end, and each rope swinger moves down a rope so that the last pair of rope swingers can join the jump line.

–Swing the rope at different speeds and heights for different skill levels.

–Have students jump with a partner.

Balance Builders

K	1	2	3	4	5	6	

 10 Min.

Level: Low

Goal: Creativity of movement and development of body awareness

Equipment: None

Formation: Scattered

Description: The teacher directs students to balance on one, two, three, four, or five body parts. The teacher then indicates that students are to move into or out of a balance while sitting, lying on the back, jumping, and so on. Students have a designated amount of time (10 seconds to 1 minute, depending on the balance) to create the balance. The first person balanced gets to select the next balance or position.

Application to gymnastics: This activity provides practice of balance positions.

–Have students work with a partner to practice before performing the balances with a time limit.

–Designate the type of balance, such as an upright or semi-inverted balance, or name specific balances, such as arabesques, scales, or star balances.

–Have students compare and contrast balances.

–Instruct students to describe their balances to the class.

–Do not perform inverted balances if you do not have mats.

–For balances with partners, make sure all students understand safety considerations. Safety reminders include not performing a balance that both partners can't do and avoiding balances in which one student bears the majority of the partner's weight in such a way that one could get injured.

–Review positions and balances that students will be performing or using to create a balance.

–Assess students quickly (in under 20 seconds, if possible) so that they don't hold a balance too long.

Have students create a balance with a partner, then have them describe the balance so that the rest of the class can perform it too.

It's on the Line

| K | 1 | 2 | 3 | 4 | 5 | 6 | 7 | 8 |

15-20 Min.

Level: Low-High

Goal: To practice basic locomotor and gymnastics motor skills, such as headstand, jump turn, or cartwheel

Equipment: Light-colored vinyl (or other material) cutouts arranged in a line

Formation: Small groups (five to eight children) per line sequence

Description: The line sequence illustrated requires students to use a variety of skills and numerous changes of direction. Students must determine how to match their hands, feet, head, or other body part to the shapes on the puzzle and then determine the skill to perform and the direction to move in. For example, in the first stretch of the puzzle course in the diagram, the student would walk, do a quarter turn right, take a step backward, jump backward, jump and turn left. The object is to move through the puzzle as quickly and accurately as possible.

Application to gymnastics: This activity reinforces basic gymnastics skills and challenges students' ability to perform transitions from one type of skill to another.

–Set up the line sequences using tasks that reflect the skill level and comprehension of the students.

–Review what each of the symbols represents before students begin the line sequence.

–Set up as many lines as necessary (and as room allows) to allow activity of as many students as possible.

 –Make sure that activities requiring inverted balances are performed on a matted surface.

–Make sure that there is ample space between lines so that students don't run into each other.

 Have enough courses set up that no more than eight students work at each course.

 –Set a time limit for completing the course, and vary the time limit.

–When setting up each line sequence, group similar skills together (jumps, balances, etc.).

–Have students with stopwatches at each line keep time as students progress through each sequence.

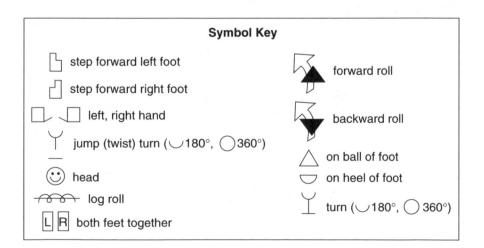

Hold It

| 1 | 2 | 3 | 4 |

10 Min.

Level: Low-Medium

Goal: To balance on a variety of large and small body parts in upright, inverted, symmetrical, and asymmetrical positions using good form; to know several classic balance positions as well as to invent solutions to balance problems; to develop a simple balance sequence—balance, weight transfer, balance

Equipment: Matted floor area

Formation: Scattered

Description: The teacher shows children pictures of a variety of classic balance poses (such as front support, back support, tuck, pike, tip-up, headstand) and names them. Students try several of the poses, holding them for three to five seconds. The teacher talks about balancing on a variety of body parts (hands, feet, knees, tummy, seat, shoulder, etc.) and has the students demonstrate several balances using these different parts. The students choose two of their favorite or best balances and link them in a short sequence.

Application to gymnastics: Students practice balances and transitional movements that are central to gymnastics performance.

–Make sure all students understand the terminology: the names of the skills, how skills should look, and how to perform them.

–Logical forms of weight transfer must be used to make transitions—smooth rolls, sliding actions, steps, and so on. Hold balances to show a clear beginning and ending.

–Use tasks that will challenge but not frustrate the students. Use the sequencing task as a way to assess students' knowledge and understanding of the skills learned.

–Show pictures of each skill, or have a student demonstrate each skill as you explain it.

–Have students tell the performance points of each skill as they perform it.

–Any balances in an inverted position must be performed on panel mats.

–Mat the entire area students will be using. If you have panel mats, arrange them in as large a square as possible.

–Provide many opportunities to practice individual skills before having students combine them into sequences.

–Creativity is of primary importance here!

–Vary the tasks to be performed or the type of sequence to be developed.

–Have the children invent new balance poses by varying the number of body parts used for support, the level of the body during balance, the width of body, the shape of body (straight, curved, twisted), body symmetry or asymmetry, and orientation (upright or inverted). Combine two of these factors simultaneously (e.g., wide and symmetrical, inverted and straight).

Partner Balances

3 4 5 6

 20 Min.

Level: Med-High

Goal: To examine the principles of counterbalance and counter-tension

Equipment: Strip or panel mats arranged in a square, pictures of various balances

Formation: Scattered on mats

Description: The instructor begins by showing the students pictures of several partner balances. The instructor then demonstrates one or two partner balances and explains the principles of good balance and supporting another person's weight. Each student chooses a partner and a work space. Each pair should try several different partner balances, the ones pictured as well as ones they invent themselves. After choosing one balance they like or can do best, they begin by having one partner assume an individual balance of his or her choice.

Then, using a weight transfer action of his or her choice (such as a roll, cartwheel, step, or jump) this student approaches the partner, and they move into the partner balance with a smooth, logical transition. After holding the partner balance for three to five seconds, the second student chooses another transitional action to move away and finishes in a second individual balance. The sequence is pose, transition, partner balance, transition, pose. Finally, the pair chooses two or three partner balances and develops a longer sequence.

Application to gymnastics: Students learn and practice more difficult balances and more challenging ways of moving into and out of those balances, both individually and with a partner.

–Have students practice partner balances before putting them into sequence activities.

–Select partners based on their strengths, weaknesses, and ability to work together.

–When students choose their own partners, encourage them to select a partner wisely, based on ability level, body size, and weight, with whom they can work productively.

–Have students experiment with a variety of balances before choosing the ones they will use in their sequences. Both partners must be able to perform the balances.

–Be sure that the area where students will be working is matted or that the balances they will be performing do not require mats.

–Be careful that partners are equitably matched for strength and size.

–Remind all students about general and personal space, and make sure that these concepts are safely put into practice.

–Creativity is of primary importance here!

–There are no right or wrong solutions to the partner balances.

–Make cards with the names and pictures of balances and arrange them by type. Have students draw a card from each category and create a balance sequence.

–For a more complex challenge, set a time limit for developing and performing the sequences.

22 Balance Puzzles

 10-20
Min.

Level: Low

Goal: To practice static balances

Equipment: Body part shapes drawn on cardboard or other material, panel mats

Formation: Scattered

Description: Prior to class time, the instructor draws balance puzzle charts (see illustrations) with markers on sheets of paper, poster board, or cardboard. The charts may be laminated for better durability. Beginning with the easier puzzles, the instructor holds up one chart at a time and asks the children to balance on the body parts shown. The children must balance on the correct parts in the position shown in the chart, with no other body parts touching the floor.

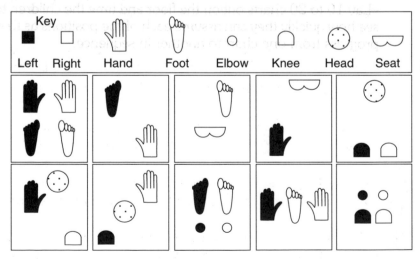

From *Perceptual Motor Development*, Peter Werner. Copyright © 1976, John Wiley & Sons, Inc. Reprinted by permission of John Wiley & Sons, Inc.

Application to gymnastics: Static balances help children learn body awareness and spatial orientation. Balance puzzles challenge children to use visual decoding, association, and memory and teach them to solve static balance problems.

–Be prepared to reinforce the concepts of right and left and of static balance. Don't move when in a position of balance!

–As children perform each puzzle, have them say aloud each body part involved.

–If needed, arrange panel mats in a large square on which children can do balances.

–Reinforce the concepts of personal and general space.

–Make the puzzle charts large so all students can see them.

–If necessary, make several copies of the puzzles so that more than one area can be used.

–Show the children one to four charts and then remove them from their vision. Ask the children to use their visual memory to assume the balance position (or sequence of positions) shown.

–Lay 10 to 20 charts out on the floor and time the children to see how quickly they can assume each of the positions as they progress from one chart to another in sequence.

Alphabet Soup

| 2 | 3 | 4 | 5 |

 7-10 Min.

Level: Low-Medium

Goal: Creativity, practice of basic gymnastics positions and balances

Equipment: Floor exercise mat or panel mats arranged in a large square

Formation: Scattered

Description: Players move randomly around the floor using a gymnastics motor skill (such as leap, skip, chassé, roll) or any locomotor skill. When the instructor calls out a letter of the alphabet, students form groups of three. Using gymnastics balancing skills, each group forms the shape of the letter and holds it until the instructor calls "alphabet soup." Students then resume moving about until the instructor calls out the next letter.

Application to gymnastics: Students practice gymnastics positions, balances, and motor and locomotor skills.

–Review the various balances that can be used to form letters.

–Review gymnastics positions that can form part of the letters (such as a bridge for part of an "h").

–Easier letters are A, C, D, E, F, H, I, K, L, N, T, U, V, Y, Z.

–More difficult letters are B, G, J, M, O, P, Q, R, S, W, X.

–Students can lie on the floor to form letters, but encourage them to be more creative.

–Students can form upper- or lowercase letters (teacher can designate which to perform).

–Reinforce the concepts of general and personal space.

–Use mats if skills such as rolls are used for moving around or if inverted balances are used.

–Modify the size of the groups so that no students are left out.

–To prevent the same students from always working together, have students choose different groups each time a new letter is called.

–Have groups form different letters to spell out words.

–Have students draw a letter out of a hat, but don't let them look at the letter until you give the signal for the letter to be formed.

24 Stone, Bridge, and Tree

K	1	2	3	

 10 Min.

Level: Low-Medium

Goal: To reinforce locomotor and basic gymnastics skills

Equipment: Panel mats, floor beam (if available)

Formation: Lines (four to five students per line)

Description: In each group, one student is designated as a "stone," one is a "bridge," and one is a "tree." The remaining students are runners. The stone assumes a tuck on the floor; the bridge assumes a bridge or a straddle either standing upright or with hands on the floor in front of feet; the tree stands upright with feet together and arms extended straight overhead. On a signal from the instructor, the first runner skips to the stone, jumps over the stone, leaps to the bridge, crawls under the bridge, runs around the tree, and then performs a gymnastics locomotor skill back to take the place of the stone. The stone replaces the bridge, the bridge replaces the tree, and the tree becomes a runner. Students continue until all have had a turn in each position.

Application to gymnastics: Various gymnastics motor and loco-motor skills are reinforced with this activity.

Stone

Bridge

Tree

–Review all skills in the activity before students perform them. Show the students pictures of each skill to be used.

–Remind students that the object is not to be finished first, but to have completed all the skills correctly and in good form.

 –Make sure each group has plenty of room to perform in so that they don't get in the way of another group.

–Be sure all students are able to perform the skills selected.

–Reinforce concepts of general and personal space to prevent accidents.

 Although this activity is a relay, students should be reminded to work together as a team, particularly to remind each other about moving from one "object" to the next.

 –Use skills from warm-up activities or body preparation drills as part of the line activities.

–Add more skills to the sequence to make the line more challenging.

25

Footsie Rolls

	2	3	4	5	6	

10 Min.

Level: Low

Goal: Partner cooperation and synchronization for rolls

Equipment: Matted surface (floor exercise mat or panel mats arranged in lines)

Formation: Paired lines

Description: The instructor demonstrates a log roll (or pencil roll) to the students and allows them to practice the skill. Once children have mastered the roll, the instructor challenges them to perform it in pairs, lying on their backs with the soles of their feet together. The object of the activity is for partners to roll as far as they can without breaking foot contact. Once the connection is broken, another pair takes a turn.

Application to gymnastics: Children practice the basic skill of side rolling, extending their knowledge and performance ability.

–Stress that the aim of the activity is to not break the connection.

–Use as much space as possible so as many pairs can perform as possible.

–Remind students about how to roll in a straight line with a log roll: The body position should be hollow (stomach and upper chest rounded), with feet and shoulders rolling simultaneously.

–Students should roll on mats to avoid hurting their hip bones on the floor.

–Students should be far enough apart that they will not run into another rolling pair if they don't roll in a straight line.

Finishing first is not the goal! It is hard to roll fast and be first but still stay in contact.

–Try rolling as one long human chain by having students roll together head to foot.

–Form roller tag teams: Students form groups of three, and two roll as a pair. After a certain distance has been covered, one of the rollers is replaced by the third member of the team.

–Have students lie with hands instead of feet together, holding hands as they roll.

26

Shapes

| | 3 | 4 | 5 | 6 | |

 10 Min.

Level: Low

Goal: To reinforce basic gymnastics jumps and turns and to understand the shapes made by performing these skills

Equipment: None

Formation: Scattered

Description: Students begin with random running, leaping, skipping, or other locomotor skill. When the instructor calls "jump," students jump into the air to create a shape of their choice or one that the teacher calls out. Some sample jumps are straddle, tuck, frog, stag, dolphin (straight jump), split, pike, half twist, full twist, arch, and star.

Application to gymnastics: Students practice gymnastics skills and learn about the shapes their bodies make when performing these skills, which can help them develop aesthetically pleasing gymnastics routines.

Sailor

Straddle Jump

Split Jump

Bird

–Review all skills that will be performed before assessing students on them.

–Demonstrate or show pictures with the names of the skills as you review the important performance points for each skill.

Remind students about the concepts of general and personal space so they can avoid running into each other.

Select skills to be performed appropriately for the skill level of the students.

–Allow students to choose the skill to be performed.

–Perform two or three jumps in sequence. Prepare cards that show a variety of jumps, one jump to a card. Two or three students each draw a card. When the teacher says "jump," those students show their cards to the class, and the remaining students perform the series of jumps in the sequence shown.

Run-Jump-Land

K	1	2	3	

 10 Min.

Level: Low

Goal: To reinforce gymnastics jumping and landing skills

Equipment: Matted floor area

Formation: Scattered

Description: The instructor indicates the locomotor skill to be used (e.g., run, skip, hop, chassé). Students begin to move around the designated area using the indicated locomotor skill when the instructor gives the starting signal. When teacher calls out "jump-land!", all students immediately jump into the air and try to "stick" their landing, that is, land with good form in a stable position. Their goal is to try not to wobble or lose balance when they land.

Application to gymnastics: This activity is excellent for reinforcing the importance of proper landings, which are critical to gymnastics performance. It is also good for practicing various gymnastics jumps.

–Review the mechanics of good landing: knees slightly flexed, body leaning slightly forward with weight over legs, feet slightly apart, land on balls of feet. Students should repeat aloud the performance cues for safe landings.

–Cue students with cards or pictures of the specific jump you want them to perform.

–Be lenient with wobbles if children are just beginning to work on performing good landings.

Make sure students understand that they should land on their feet; they are not to fall down unless specifically told to. In this activity, a fall would be cause to start over.

Use this activity as a review, and keep it short.

–Allow children to select the jump to perform.

–Play the game Mother May I? using jumps. If children wobble or fall over they must go back to the starting line.

–Scatter folded panel mats around, and have students jump from one mat to another. (Be sure to pick some students to hold the mats down securely.)

Balance Tag

1	2	3	4		

 10 Min.

Level: Low

Goal: To practice body control and balance skills

Equipment: None

Formation: Scattered

Description: The teacher selects a student to be "it." All other students are scattered around the playing area. On the word "go," all students begin to move around the area using various locomotor skills designated by either the teacher or the person who is "it." "It" tries to tag as many players as possible. Players are safe only when in a balance position specified by "it" or the teacher. When tagged, players join "it" as taggers.

Application to gymnastics: This activity provides good practice for static balance skills and locomotor movements.

–Allow time for the students to practice the balances before using them in the game.

–Develop a system for selecting the person to be "it."

–Show cards with various balances to be selected at the beginning of the game and leave them visible for reference by the students during the game if necessary.

–Do not use inverted balances in this activity.

–Remind students to watch where they move in the game so that they don't run into each other.

–Let the students select the locomotor skill to be used for moving around.

–Set a time limit for being "it."

–Let students do balances with partners or in groups of three.

29 Barracuda Barricade

 10 Min.

Level: Low

Goal: To practice gymnastics and locomotor skills

Equipment: Panel mats, rubber circles (dots)

Formation: Scattered

Description: Spread panel mats out on the floor exercise mat or gym floor at different angles with about 12 to 18 inches (30-45 centimeters) between mats. The panel mats are "land," the circles (dots) are "islands," and the surrounding area is the "water." Two students are the barracudas and must stay in the water. The remaining students stay on the mats as "landlubbers." On the word "go," the barracudas swim in the water and try to catch the landlubbers. The barracudas can reach or jump over the panel mats to tag landlubbers, but they cannot step on the land. If they do, they must join the landlubbers. Landlubbers try to avoid the barracudas by jumping from mat to mat. They cannot touch the water or the barracudas. If they do, they become barracudas. All barracudas work together to catch the landlubbers. The last two players caught become the starting barracudas in the next game.

Application to gymnastics: This activity is good for practicing locomotor skills. Variations allow practicing other gymnastics skills, such as cartwheels or stride leaps.

–The mats should be close enough that students will not have a problem moving among them.

–Let students select the skills used to move over land (from mat to mat). Allow students time to practice the skills before using them in the game.

 –Remind students about general and personal space and rules for moving around in that space.

–If mats slide on the floor, use tape or other means to hold them securely in place.

 –This game is one that needs to move quickly.

–Vary the amount of time for barracudas to catch people.

 –Occasionally the teacher can call "freeze," and all students must stop in a balance position. Students can also do partner or group balances or arabesques when tagged by a barracuda.

–Vary the locomotor skills (e.g., cartwheels, rolls, stride leaps) used to travel around the playing area.

30

Red Light, Green Light

| K | 1 | 2 | 3 | 4 | |

5
Min.

Level: Low

Goal: Basic locomotor skills practice

Equipment: Floor mat or panel mats arranged in a large square

Formation: Scattered

Description: Place mats in a large square. Students line up at one end of the mats, with the teacher at the "police station" at the other end. The "police officer" calls out either "green light" and the name of a skill (for example, "green light, cartwheel") or "red light." On a green light command, the students move toward the police station by performing the indicated skill; on a red light command, they must freeze. Students who move during a red light or those who perform an incorrect skill go back to the beginning. The game continues until one student reaches the police station.

Application to gymnastics: Students practice locomotor and gymnastics skills.

–Make sure the skills to be performed are selected appropriately for the performance level of the students.

–Review all skills to be performed so that students understand and are able to perform the designated skills.

 Be sure area is clear and sufficient space is available for safe group movement in the same direction.

 Be lenient on the "freeze" command!

 Vary the skills to be performed.

Stunt Relays

	2	3	4	5	6	

5-10 Min.

Level: Medium

Goal: To practice leaps, jumps, and basic gymnastics skills

Equipment: Panel mats arranged in a large square, other equipment determined by individual tasks, stickers or other small prizes

Formation: Small groups at stations

Description: Create a jump relay race course with four stations and as many teams as needed for everyone to participate. One station is set up at each corner of a 40-by-40-foot (12-by-12-meter) mat (area depends on gym size). Each team member has to complete the course and tag the next person in line until everyone on the team has taken a turn. The first team to finish the entire course by performing all skills correctly wins a small prize. Team members must finish in line with their hands on hips to be eligible to win.

Station	Skill
1	Three leaps
2	One forward roll
3	Your favorite jump
4	Cartwheel

Application to gymnastics: This is an excellent opportunity for students to practice a variety of specific gymnastics skills in a setting that requires them to move quickly but accurately.

 −Be sure teams are matched by ability and age.

−Assess student performance based on the key parts of the skill being performed. Make sure the skills to be performed are selected based on the performance level of the students.

−Review all terminology and all skills to be performed to be sure that students understand and are able to perform the designated skills.

−Set up a criteria sheet for successful completion of the tasks, and make sure students understand the criteria.

−Remind students that the object is not only to be finished first, but to have completed all the skills correctly and in good form.

 Make sure that all students understand about general and personal space and that the concepts are reinforced throughout the activity.

 Be sure to walk through the course for the activities to be sure students are familiar with the tasks to be performed as well as the order in which to perform them.

 −This activity lends itself to many excellent variations.

−Increase skill difficulty as skill level increases.

−Have a student select the skill to be performed at each station.

Four Corners, Four Poses

| 2 | 3 | 4 | 5 | 6 |

 10 Min.

Level: Medium

Goal: Skill development

Equipment: Large mattted area or panel mats arranged in a square

Formation: Scattered

Description: One person is selected to be blindfolded in the middle. All others skip, chassé, or do another gymnastics locomotor skill around the mat. The blindfolded person calls "stop" then counts to 10. All students quickly move to one of the four corners of the mat and assume the pose designated at that corner (knee scale, headstand, handstand, pike-straddle stand, etc.). The blindfolded person calls out one of the designated poses, removes the blindfold, and picks the next person to be blindfolded from those who were in the designated corner. Instruct students that they must move through each corner before they repeat a pose.

Application to gymnastics: Students practice selected balance skills, which are an important part of gymnastics routines.

–Make sure the skills are selected based on the performance level of the students.

–Review all skills to be performed to be sure that students understand and are able to perform them.

 –Be sure the blindfolded person remains stationary or is protected from the others' movements while blindfolded.

–Instruct students not to move through the blindfolded student's area.

 Select the poses to focus on skills that the group needs to improve. Skills from compulsory routines or poses work well here.

 Focus only on flexibility skills.

Keep It Up!

 5-7 Min.

Level: Medium

Goal: To practice selected gymnastics jumps and locomotor skills

Equipment: Balloons or beach balls

Formation: Scattered

Description: Students see how many times they can hit a balloon or a beach ball to keep it up in the air while doing a gymnastics or locomotor skill (full twist jump, backward roll, cartwheel, leap, chassé, etc.) between each hit. This can be a contest between individual students or between teams. A point is scored each time the balloon is hit in the air, a skill is performed, and the balloon is hit again. If the balloon touches the floor or another student, the count starts over.

Application to gymnastics: This is an extension activity for practicing selected gymnastics skills.

–Assess student performance based on the key parts of the skill.

–Make sure the skills to be performed are selected appropriately for the performance level of the students.

–Review all performance cues for selected skills with the students. Make sure all students understand the names of the skills, how skills should look, and how to perform them.

–Have pictures to illustrate each skill, or have a student demonstrate each skill as you explain it.

–Students must stay on the matted area for the skill performed to count in their scores.

–Make sure the object to keep aloft is light, such as a beach ball or balloon.

–Make sure students stay in their own area.

Students are on the honor system for keeping score.

–Do a different gymnastics skill after each balloon hit.

–Allow students to select skills to be performed.

–Perform a sequence of skills, such as straight jump, straddle jump, forward roll, or balance.

–See how many skills can be done correctly before the balloon touches the floor.

–Teams can compete by challenging each other to perform a specified skill. One player performs the skill. If the balloon touches the floor, the other team gets the point and the next player takes a turn.

–Instead of points, players are awarded letters. The first player to spell the phrase *Keep it up!* is the winner.

34 **Balloon Relay Race**

K	1	2	3	4	

8 Min.

Level: Low-Medium

Goal: Gymnastics skill development

Equipment: Balloons, floor mat or panel mats arranged in a large square with marked starting and finish lines

Formation: Lines

Description: The instructor separates the class into two or more teams. At the starting line, the first student on each team hits the balloon, performs a skill designated by the instructor (such as a log roll, forward roll, or cartwheel) while the balloon is aloft, then catches the balloon. Students continue in this manner until they reach the finish line. Then they run back to the starting line and hand the balloon to the next student on their team, who repeats the performance.

Application to gymnastics: Students practice specific gymnastics skills.

–Make sure the skills to be performed are selected appropriately for the performance level of the students.

–Review all skills to be performed to be sure that students understand and are able to perform them.

–Use tasks that will challenge but not frustrate the students.

 Make sure students remember to stay in their own area and to pass the balloon gently to each other.

 Remind students of the importance of finishing the skill before hitting the balloon.

 –Students do combinations of skills before hitting the balloon.

–Change the skill after each hit (for example, first hit, log roll; second hit, cartwheel; third hit, backward roll; fourth hit, jump tuck).

Spaghetti Bodies

K	1	2	3	4	5	6	

 5 Min.

Level: Low

Goal: To help students become kinesthetically aware of whole-body muscular tension

Equipment: Panel mats

Formation: Scattered pairs

Description: Students work in pairs. One partner assumes a basic static shape, and the other partner tests for a "loose body" by attempting to separate legs, break the body line, open or close the hip angle, and so on.

Application to gymnastics: This activity helps students recognize internal tightness of muscles. Since many gymnastics skills require muscular tension, the goal is for students to become rigid, like uncooked rather than cooked spaghetti. The ability to identify muscular tension is a kinesthetic skill that is transferable to physical activities children will do later in life.

Demonstrate this activity well so that students understand the purpose of the activity and can do it with a partner.

 Do not push on students' lower backs.

 Remind students that the idea of the activity is to help their partners identify muscular tightness, not to knock them over.

 –Have students perform shoulder stands while partners grasp their feet and ankles and try to shake their bodies loose.

–For more advanced students, have them try to assume taut balance poses.

36

Cupcake Walk

| | 2 | 3 | 4 | 5 | 6 | |

 10 Min.

Level: Medium

Goal: To practice gymnastics skills

Equipment: Paper plates, slips of paper with gymnastics skills in a hat or bowl, matted floor area, cupcakes or small prizes

Formation: Circle

Description: Paper plates are arranged in a circle, one for each student plus 5 to 10 extra plates. About one-fifth of the plates should have an illustration of a cupcake (or appropriate prize). Before class, the teacher prints gymnastics skills on slips of paper and puts them in a hat. Three slips should read "stop." To begin the game, students stand in a circle, each behind a plate. The teacher draws a slip and reads the skill aloud. Each student must perform the skill in a clockwise direction around the circle, advancing to the next plate. Continue in this manner until a slip reading "stop" is drawn. At this point, every student standing next to a cupcake plate wins a prize.

Application to gymnastics: This game is a fun way for students to practice specific gymnastics skills in a format with which many of them may be familiar from school carnivals.

84

–This game works well as a review of dance skill terms, such as waltz step, chassé, hitch kick, and cat leap.

–Use tasks that will challenge but not frustrate the students. Use low-complexity skills for beginners (locomotor skills, basic rolls, etc.) and more difficult skills for more advanced students.

–Show pictures of each skill, or have a student demonstrate each skill as you explain it.

–Set up a criteria sheet of key performance points for assessing successful completion of the skills, and make sure students understand the criteria.

–Place the plates at a sufficient distance from each other to avoid collisions. Students should avoid stepping on the plates but should stand next to or behind the plate instead.

–If rolling skills are used, be sure the entire area is matted.

Be sure to provide 5 to 10 more plates than the number of students in class.

–Vary the tasks to be performed each time children go around the circle. This game can be used for building strength with handstand walking, crab walking, and backbend walking.

–Instead of cupcakes, rewards such as stickers and stamps work well.

37

Mirror! Mirror!

 10 Min.

Level: Medium

Goal: To practice mirroring a skill

Equipment: Variety of equipment as required by specific activities

Formation: Stations or scattered pairs

Description: Each student copies the actions or jumps of the teacher or, working in pairs, mirrors the actions or jumps of a partner.

Application to gymnastics: Students practice gymnastics skills on both right and left sides of the body, which is important for future performance. This activity also increases students' movement vocabulary.

–Make sure the skills to be performed are selected appropriately for the performance level of the students.

–Review all performance cues for the skills you have selected.

–Use tasks that will challenge but not frustrate the students.

–Show pictures of each skill, or have a student demonstrate each skill as you explain it before the game.

 Make sure you have enough space to allow a variety of skills to be used and to prevent collisions.

 Be sure to remind students to choose tasks for mirroring that are within both their own and their partners' abilities.

 –Vary the tasks to be performed, using many movement types. Focus on one class of skills, such as jumps, or on one specific skill. Variations in movement will enhance students' adaptability and kinesthetic awareness.

–Mirror a series of skills to a certain rhythm or song, then do the same series to a very different rhythm. This is a good way for students to focus on how rhythm affects the movement.

–Use reverse imaging. That is, instead of mirroring each other (one partner moves left while the other moves right), each partner moves to his or her respective left or right, away from each other.

International Olympiad

| | 2 | 3 | 4 | 5 | 6 | |

 20 Min.

Level: Low-High

Goal: Practice in finishing skills, cooperation, and working as a team

Equipment: Matted floor area, other equipment as available

Formation: Lines

Description: Students form lines that represent gymnastics teams from different countries. The teacher starts by telling the story of a young gymnast who is new to the team (who can be played by one of the students in the class) who has difficulty finishing skills and landing properly. The teacher or a student demonstrates how skills were incorrectly performed. It is each team's responsibility to help this new teammate learn about the proper way to finish skills. Assign a sequence of skills that are to be performed with proper finishing techniques. The team members must add finishing techniques and help each other and the new team member perform these skills to the best of their abilities by providing performance cues and feedback. For each skill completed properly, points are awarded to the team. The team with the highest score selects the next sequence of skills to perform.

Application to gymnastics: Students practice tumbling skills and finishing techniques, which are very important to successful execution of gymnastics skills.

–Allow students to practice the skills prior to the International Olympiad.
–Students should review important performance points for each skill before performing it.
–Select skills that students can do successfully.

Check spacing of groups to avoid collisions.

Keep the skills at an appropriate level for the students' performance ability.

–Make large cards with the names and pictures of the skills.
–Other teams can critique skill performance.

Add-On

 | **2** | **3** | **4** | **5** | **6** |

 10 Min.

Level: Low

Goal: To practice skills in new or different sequences

Equipment: Mats, any event apparatus

Formation: Varies by task

Description: This is a classic gymnastics game in which one student performs a skill, the next student repeats the skill and adds another to it, the third student adds a third skill to the sequence, and so on. The game can be played using any gymnastics event that requires movement sequencing.

Application to gymnastics: This activity aids in skill development, requires remembering skills sequences, and encourages creativity, all of which are necessary for creating gymnastics routines.

–Make sure the skills to be performed are selected appropriately for the performance level of all the students.

–Use this activity to make skill drills more interesting.

Attempting new skills in sequence can be challenging. Be sure skills are ones that students have mastered so that the challenge rests on sequencing the skills, not on performing them.

Remind students that the object is not to be finished first, but to have completed all the skills correctly and in good form.

Focus on themes such as balances, strength skills, and so on.

Conditioning and Endurance Games and Activities

40

Over the Rope

10 Min.

Level: Medium

Goal: To develop shoulder and abdominal strength and control

Equipment: Hoops, ropes, or bungee cord; horizontal bar with mats beneath

Formation: Single-file line per station

Description: The teacher holds the hoop or rope in front of a low horizontal bar. The student does an underswing dismount or sole circle dismount through the hoop or over the rope to a stand. The teacher progressively raises the hoop or rope to encourage more height on the landing.

Application to gymnastics: This activity helps develop height and control of bar underswing and sole circle dismounts. It also promotes control of swinging skills. Students learn to swing under and away from a bar and to lift hips and legs to swing over an object.

–Be sure to raise the level of the rope or hoop as students learn the technique of the swing.

–Show pictures of the skill, or have a student demonstrate the skill as you explain it.

–Students can assist by holding the rope.

–Once the students are successful at getting over the rope, focus their attention on the quality of their performance (keeping legs straight, solid and controlled landings, etc.).

–Use mats under the bar.

–Adjust the height of the rope for each student's ability level.

Remind students that the object is not only to get through the hoop or over the rope, but to do so using good form.

–Award points for each solid landing.

–Assign students to teams, and set a time limit. The team with the most points at the end of the period wins, or play until one team scores a specified number of points.

41

Swing and Glide

K	1	2	3	4	5	6	

20
Min.

Level: Medium-High

Goal: To develop swinging form and strength

Equipment: Beanbag or foam object, bars to swing on, mats under bars

Formation: Lines

Description: The first student places a beanbag or foam block between the knees or ankles and performs a swinging skill on the bars (e.g., swinging back and forth, swing half turn, underswing) while trying to keep the object in place. If the student successfully completes the skill, the next student attempts that skill and adds another skill. Each successive student attempts the preceding sequence and, if successful, adds a new skill to the sequence. Each student who completes the sequence correctly is awarded a letter in the word *gymnastics*. The first person or team to spell *gymnastics* wins. Ties can be broken by a swing-off in which each student has a chance to perform.

Application to gymnastics: Students develop good swinging form in this activity.

–Review the performance components of skills before students attempt them. Select the skills appropriately for the performance level of the students. Check that all students understand the names of the skills, how skills should look, and how to perform them.

–Use tasks that will challenge but not frustrate the students. Remember that swinging skills are more difficult than other skills because they require more strength.

–Show pictures of each skill, or have a student demonstrate each skill as you explain it.

–Use key performance points of the skills as the criteria for successful completion, and make sure students understand the criteria.

–Lower skill level students can touch the floor between swings.

Use adequate and proper matting under the bar. Students should always use safe landing skills.

–Keep legs and body tight.
–Correct body positions are a must!

Dismount over a rope, dropping the beanbag before landing but after completion of the skill.

42 Wall Walk

| | | **5** | **6** | **7** | **8** |

10
Min.

Level: High

Goal: To develop shoulder strength

Equipment: Wall, panel mats arranged next to wall

Formation: Pairs

Description: From a front support (push-up) position with soles of feet against the wall, the student walks his or her feet up the wall to a mark or line and back down. (The mark should be at a height such that the student's body forms an angle of about 45 degrees with the floor when his or her feet reach the mark.) Repeat a total of three times. A partner should assist if necessary by holding the waist of the student who is walking up the wall. Students should try to keep their bodies extended and heads in line with the body when moving their feet up and down the wall.

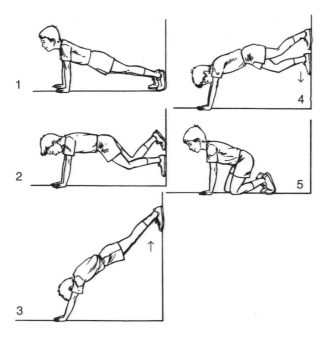

Application to gymnastics: This activity develops shoulder strength, which is necessary to perform handstands and skills that require pushing off a surface (such as roundoffs or vaulting skills).

–Review the performance points of the skills to be performed to be sure that students understand and are able to perform the designated skills.

–Use key performance points as the criteria for assessing successful completion of the tasks, and be sure students understand the criteria.

–Matting is required for this activity. Have students stand on the ends of the mats to hold them in place if the mats begin to slide.

–Students can work with partners to spot and assist each other. Adequate space should be provided between pairs of students to minimize the risk of injury from collisions.

Students should walk up the wall only as high as their ability allows (determined by their shoulder strength and skill level) and never higher than the mark.

43

Stiff Along Walk

 5 Min.

Level: High

Goal: To improve shoulder strength and flexibility

Equipment: Floor exercise or wrestling mats or panel mats arranged in a square

Formation: Lines

Description: Students place their hands on the mats approximately two to three feet (60-90 centimeters) in front of their feet, depending on their height. Students bend at the waist and lift both feet off the mat at the same time, shifting their weight from the feet to the hands, then place their feet back on the mat close to their hands. Students repeat this movement forward across the mat.

Application to gymnastics: This activity develops shoulder and back strength for performing press skills.

–Students should keep arms and legs stiff.

–Students should review the performance cues for this skill.

–Show pictures of this skill, or have a student demonstrate as you explain it.

–Remind students that the object is not to be finished first, but to perform the skill correctly and in good form.

 Remind students to keep arms extended—not to bend their elbows. They need to be able to support themselves, and bending the elbows could cause them to fall forward.

 Remind students to place their feet only as close to their hands as feels comfortable. They know how flexible their own backs are.

 –Students can do the skill backward.

–Spread the legs and move in a pike-straddle position.

Cross the Alligator Pit

 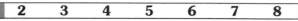

| | 2 | 3 | 4 | 5 | 6 | 7 | 8 |

 10-20 Min.

Level: Low-High (depending on set-up of the pit)

Goals: To improve agility, to stretch out the body, and to promote cooperation

Equipment: Matted floor area, targets (tape marks or other indicators), various gymnastics equipment (wedge mats, beams, or other equipment that can be used in the manner described)

Formation: Teams of students (size of teams based on class size and available space)

Description: Equipment is arranged so that students can move safely from target to target on or over the equipment from a starting point to a finish point. Equipment and targets are set up so that team members will have to work together to get from a target to a piece of equipment. The targets and equipment are arranged around the floor with enough space between them that students must jump, leap, or stretch to get to the next area. Team members help each other by providing a reaching assist, helping maintain balance upon landing, helping cross the equipment (lifting, pulling, pushing, supporting each other), etc. Designate how each piece of equipment is to be crossed (by climbing over, crawling under, swinging under, walking across, etc.). The space between targets and equipment is the "alligator pit." The object of the activity is to avoid the alligator pit (with help from team members) from the time the activity starts (on command of teacher) until it ends (when students reach the last target or piece of equipment and can reach the end of the pit in safety). Targets and equipment must be crossed in the order designated by the teacher.

Application to gymnastics: Students work on stretching the body from the beginning to the end of a skill as they move from equipment to targets. This activity also promotes teamwork.

 –Select the skills to be performed in the game based on the performance level of the students. Be sure not to make skills so difficult that students become frustrated.

–Check that all students understand the names of the skills, how skills should look, and how to perform them.

–Show pictures of each skill, or have a student demonstrate each skill as you explain it.

 Use proper and adequate matting.

 Stress that this is a cooperative activity!

 The game can be varied depending on the available equipment and the students' abilities. For example, if you have a set of bars, you can use variations of swinging skills. If wedge mats are available, you can have students roll up and down the mat.

Springing Circuits

		5	6	7	8

5 Min.

Level: Medium-High

Goal: To condition leg muscles

Equipment: Matted floor area with various stations set up as circuits for springing over. These can include circuits with cones or foam cubes to spring over, carpet squares to spring to or over, panel mats arranged so that part of the mat is elevated and must be sprung over, etc.

Formation: Lines, with teacher designating starting point for each student

Description: Springing circuits are arranged so students will alternate stations, moving from two feet to two feet to the next station where they move from one foot to two feet. A variety of stations can be used. Two are shown below. Students should number off according to the number of stations used. Beginning at the station corresponding to the students' number (and moving through the circuit to each higher num-ber), students move through the springing activities. Emphasis is on proper take-off and landing and following the foot sequence indicated.

Application to gymnastics: This activity reinforces the take-off and landing skills used in floor activities and vaulting.

 −Prepare a chart indicating the sequence of feet for take-off and landing.

−Make sure students land with both feet simultaneously on the two-foot landings.

 −Use adequate matting.

−Students should land with knees slightly flexed.

 Remind students not to crowd each other as they move through the circuit.

 −Change alternating foot patterns.

−Add additional stations.

−Color code stations, then have students draw sequences of colors to indicate rotation of stations.

Gymnastics Board Game

 20 Min.

Level: Low

Goal: General conditioning

Equipment: Monopoly or similar game board, one die, four or five game pieces, number cards, skill cards, skip-a-turn cards

Formation: Four to five teams

Description: Write gymnastics skills on cards and place one on each block of a game board. Make a stack of cards with a number on each, from 1 to 50. Students form four to five teams. Each team begins with two safety cards. One member of the team rolls the die and moves that

Safety space	Roll a roll	Favorite jump	Assemble	Stag leap	Arabesque	Handstand	Safety space
Roundoff							Straight jump
Chassé							Back roll
Lunge							Straddle sit
Balance							Headstand
V-seat							Tripod
Bridge							Cartwheel
Tuck jump	Safety space	Straddle jump	Front scale	Star jump	Front roll	Log roll	Safety space

number of spaces on the board. That student pulls a number card, then all members of his or her team perform the designated skill the number of times indicated on the card. A team may play one of its safety cards instead of performing the skill, but each card may be played only once during each game. The game is played for a predetermined length of time.

Application to gymnastics: This activity provides an interesting way to do conditioning work and promotes teamwork.

–Skills should be selected appropriately for the performance level of the students.

–Review all performance cues for selected skills.

–Use tasks that will challenge but not frustrate the students.

–Show pictures of each skill, or have a student demonstrate each skill as you explain it.

–Use proper matting!

–Be sure there is enough space available to perform the selected skills.

Make sure number of repetitions of each skill is appropriate for the skill level of the students.

–Use other game boards, or design one of your own.

–Vary the tasks or categories of skills (e.g., upright balances, rolls, locomotor skills) to be performed for each game.

–To play without using a game board, students can draw slips of paper with names of skills and roll a die to determine the number of repetitions to be performed.

–Keep score based on the number of correct repetitions performed.

Wheelbarrow Tag

 | 3 4 5 6 | 5 Min.

Level: Medium

Goal: To improve shoulder support strength and muscular endurance

Equipment: Matted floor area, folded panel mats

Formation: Pairs

Description: This is a tag game for pairs. Each partner assumes a front support (push-up) position with feet placed on the top surface of a folded panel mat, hands placed on the floor (see illustration). The game starts with partners at opposite ends of the panel mat. The object of the game is for the player who is "it" to try to tag the partner's hand while players walk on their hands in a front support position.

Application to gymnastics: This activity allows students to work on the shoulder strength necessary for performing inverted (and some upright) balance skills.

Review the performance cues for a correct front support position: arms straight; body tight, rigid, and straight.

 Be sure to place the folded panel mat on the matted floor area (do not place it directly on the floor).

 Monitor students for fatigue!

 Vary the height of the folded panel mat based on the skill level of the students. It can be higher for stronger and more skilled students.

48 Windshield Wipers

K	1	2	3	4	5	6	7	8

8 Min.

Level: Low

Goal: To improve overall body strength

Equipment: Matted floor area

Formation: Scattered

Description: The students work in their own personal space. Place a target or dot on the mat for each student. With their feet on the dot, students assume a front support (push-up) position. They can either hop or walk on their hands in a semicircle back and forth like windshield wipers. They must keep their feet on the target.

Application to gymnastics: This activity builds the strength necessary for working in inverted positions.

Strongly emphasize to students that they need to keep a straight-arm position, keep the body extended, and not allow their shoulders to sag.

 Make sure you keep in mind the shoulder strength of your students. Don't let them get too fatigued.

 Students need to keep their bodies rigid throughout the skill. Don't let students arch their backs or sag their shoulders.

 Have students perform a windmill by moving in a complete circle.

49

Banana Split

| | 2 | 3 | 4 | 5 | 6 | |

 5-7 Min.

Level: Low-Medium

Goal: To improve torso strength

Equipment: Matted floor area

Formation: Scattered in pairs

Description: One student assumes a hollow body position, lying on the back with feet and head off the mat. The partner rocks him or her back and forth for 10 to 30 seconds. Partners then switch places. More advanced students can also perform this activity on the stomach in an arched position.

Application to gymnastics: This activity helps students develop torso strength. It also helps reinforce the concepts of muscular tension and a tight body.

Emphasize that students should keep their stomach muscles very tight while they are doing this activity.

 Tell students to keep their heads off the mat. Remind students not to rock their partners too hard.

 Remind students that they are to keep their bodies arched in a banana shape.

 Vary the position of arms and legs.

50 Push-Up Train

		4	5	6	7	8

10 Min.

Level: Low

Goal: To develop strength and endurance

Equipment: Panel mats

Formation: Lines

Description: Students begin by lying face down in a line, head to feet. Everyone does one straight-body push-up to get into position. While pushed up, students place their feet on the shoulders of the person behind them to form a "train." After everyone is in position, students see how many push-ups they can do as a train without falling. Students also can form a circle or work in groups of four in a square. The teacher serves as "train conductor," giving instructions for the entire group to go down and up.

Application to gymnastics: This activity helps students develop shoulder strength, which is very important for working on gymnastics equipment.

–Students need to understand how important it is to keep their bodies straight and arms extended when in the up position.

–Review performance cues for push-ups to be sure all students understand them.

 –This activity should be used only with students who are able to consistently perform straight-body push-ups.

–Proceed only when all students are ready.

 Students must be able to correctly perform a straight-body push-up before they attempt this activity.

 –Students try to move the train backward and forward by walking on their hands in the up position.

–Students work in groups of four to make a "boxcar."

Handstand Hold and Walk

		6	**7**	**8**

 7 Min.

Level: High

Goal: To improve strength and balance

Equipment: Matted floor area

Formation: Scattered

Description: Students step up into a handstand position and do one of the following activities: hold the handstand without moving the hands, hold the handstand and walk on the hands for distance, or hold the handstand and stay up as long as possible in a balanced position.

Application to gymnastics: Shoulder strength and balance are necessary for inverted balances such as handstands, headstands, and shoulder stands.

Students should try to maintain good body position throughout their handstands. Assess students based on the key performance points of the skill: hollow body position; shoulders, hips, and ankles in line; head tilted backward.

–Work in pairs to assist partner in balancing, if necessary.
–Make sure adequate space is available to accommodate all students in the class.
–Only do this activity on mats.

Students need to remain in their own personal space to avoid falling into other students.

–Vary the tasks to be performed. For example, students can turn around while walking.
–Move the legs from straight and together to a straddle, stag, or pike. This makes maintaining balance more challenging.
–Students can touch the floor and go back up to the handstand if necessary.

Glossary

assemblé—Moving from one foot to both feet.

cat leap—A jump forward off one leg while swinging the other leg forward and up. Legs switch positions in midair to land on the take-off foot. The knees are bent 90 degrees while aloft.

chassé—A springing locomotor movement in which one steps forward with one leg and springs slightly off the floor, extends and closes the legs together, then lands on the back leg with the front leg raised.

doggy roll—Sideways role; starting on floor on hands and knees, roll sideways over arm and back to arm to return to starting position on hands and knees.

hitch kick—A springing locomotor movement in which one springs off the floor, simultaneously kicking one leg forward and upward. As the kicking leg returns to the floor, the other leg kicks forward and upward. Finish with both feet on the floor.

hollow body position—With stomach and upper chest rounded in a curve.

movement sequencing—Chaining or combining movements together, so that they are performed one right after the other without pausing.

pike—A position in which the upper body is bent forward at the hips.

pike-straddle stand—Standing with the legs apart and the upper body bent forward at the hips (legs remain straight).

pirouette—Turning around on one foot. This movement is also called a turn or, if in the air, a twist.

punch—An immediate jump or rebound into the air upon landing after performing a skill such as a roundoff. This rebound is important when combining skills such as roundoffs and back handsprings, because the punch puts the body in the optimal position for the next skill.

scale—A balance position in which the body is supported on one leg; the upper body is bent so the torso is parallel with the ground and the other leg is extended backward to maintain a straight line with the chest. The arms are extended in various positions.

snap-down—Quick and forceful movement of the legs from an inverted, extended position (as in a handstand) to the floor.

sole circle dismount—A bar dismount performed by casting backward to place the soles of the feet on the bar, then swinging forward under the bar, extending the legs, and releasing the bar to land standing in front of the bar.

split—A postion in which the legs are extended at an angle of 180 degrees, one forward and one backward.

star jump—A jump into the air with the legs moving to side straddle then closing together for landing, while the arms move sideways to an upward oblique position before returning to the side of the body upon landing.

straddle—A position in which the legs are extended sideways.

tuck—A position in which the body is flexed at the hips and the knees are bent and pulled up toward the chest.

underswing dismount—A bar dismount. From a front support position on top of the bar, drop the hips and swing the legs in an arc forward and under the bar, releasing the bar to land in a standing position in front of the bar.

weight transfer—Moving the body weight from one balance point to another (e.g., changing from a balance on the left foot to a balance on the right foot) in a smooth action.

Reading List

Many ideas for class activities come from talking to other teachers. It is always great to share what works well in our classes with other teachers. It is also nice to be able to share books that have good activities in them. The following books are ones that we have used and believe are good resources for your work with gymnastics and tumbling activities. The list is not all-inclusive—add your favorite titles!

CAHPER/ACSEPL. 1980. *Gymnastics: A movement approach.* Calgary, BC: Calgary Board of Education.

Gedney, J.M. 1977. *Tumbling and balancing: Basic skills and variations.* Englewood Cliffs, NJ: Prentice-Hall. (This book is out of print.)

Hacker, P.; Malmberg, E.; Nance, J.; Tilove, A.; and True, S. 1992. *Sequential gymnastics II: The instructor's guide.* 3rd ed. Indianapolis: USA Gymnastics.

Malmberg, E. 1993. *Kidnastics: A school-appropriate model for the teaching of gymnastics.* Cortland, NY: State University College at Cortland.

O'Quinn, G. 1990. *Teaching developmental gymnastics: Skills to take through life.* Austin, TX: University of Texas Press.

Schembri, G. 1983. *Aussie gym fun: A resource for schools and clubs.* Melbourne: Australian Gymnastic Federation.

———. 1983. *Introductory gymnastics: A guide for coaches and teachers.* Melbourne: Australian Gymnastic Federation.

———. 1994. *Gym skills: Youth sports resource manual for secondary schools and clubs.* Melbourne: Australian Gymnastic Federation.

Smith, G.L. 1989. *Fun stunts and tumbling stunts: An instructor's complete developmental program for students of all ages.* Byron, CA: Front Row Experience.

Szypula, G. 1970. *Tumbling and balancing for all.* Dubuque, IA: Brown.

Werner, P.H. 1994. *Teaching children gymnastics: Becoming a master teacher.* Champaign, IL: Human Kinetics.

Sample Equipment Checklist

Mats

List number and type of mats _____

_____

_____

_____

_____

_____

	Yes	No	N/A
Are mat surfaces clean and free of rips and tears?	___	___	___
Are all straps or Velcro usable?	___	___	___
Is the foam filling in landing mats in good condition?	___	___	___
Are mats stored properly?	___	___	___
Do all mats have warning or caution signs clearly visible on them?	___	___	___

Equipment

List all equipment and number of each _____

_____

_____

_____

_____

_____

_____

	Yes	No	N/A
Are all T-handles present and in good working order?	____	____	____
Are all height adjustments secure and in good working order?	____	____	____
If there are cable attachments, are they all present and in good working order?	____	____	____
Are all floor plate or leg extensions secure?	____	____	____
Are all vaulting boards free from splits, cracks, or splinters?	____	____	____
Do all pieces of equipment have warning or caution signs clearly visible on them?	____	____	____
Is all equipment stored properly?	____	____	____

Want to Contribute?

If you have an activity that you feel will really contribute to this book, please complete the form below and send it to Patty Hacker at 1814 22nd Avenue North, Brookings, SD 57006.

Focus:

❏ Warm-Up

❏ Motor/Locomotor Skill

❏ Just for Fun

❏ Strength/Endurance/Flexibility

❏ Gymnastics Skill Development

Name of Activity:

Purpose/Goal of the Activity:

Equipment Needed:

Grade Level:

Time Needed for Activity:

Complexity of Activity:

Formation for Activity:

Description of Activity:

Teaching Tips:

Safety Tips:

Variations:

Reminders:

Contributor Name, Address, and Phone:
(very important!)

About the Authors

Patty Hacker, PhD, is an associate professor of health, physical education, and recreation and coordinator of undergraduate physical-education teacher education at South Dakota State University (SDSU), Brookings. She has more than 23 years of teaching experience, 17 of them teaching physical education gymnastics and tumbling in a public-school setting. She has also conducted workshops across the United States using *Sequential Gymnastics II*, a text she coauthored.

Patty, who coached girl's gymnastics from 1974 to 1987, has judged girl's gymnastics in both high schools and private clubs since 1977. She chairs the USA Gymnastics National Education Subcommittee and is a life member of the American Association of Health, Physical Education, Recreation and Dance (AAHPERD) and a member of the South Dakota Association of Health, Physical Education, Recreation and Dance.

Patty received the SDSU Award for Teaching Excellence in 1996, was nominated for SDSU Teacher of the Year award in 1995, and received the USA Gymnastics Award for Service in 1991. She earned her doctorate in physical education pedagogy from the University of Wyoming in 1988.

Eric Malmberg, EdD, is an associate professor of physical education and coordinator of pedagogy at State University of New York College at Cortland. He has taught physical education at all levels, preschool to college, and has coached gymnastics for more than 20 years. For the past 18 years Eric has coached at the national level, allowing him to study physical education and gymnastics methodologies from around the world.

Eric is the author of *Kidnastics: A School-Appropriate Model for the Teaching of*

Gymnastics, a book that combines educational gymnastics and traditional gymnastics into a safe and easy-to-implement teaching method for physical educators.

As a college gymnastics coach, Eric was a four-time winner of the National College Coach of the Year for NCAA Division II and III men's gymnastics. He is a member of AAHPERD and the USA Gymnastics Education Subcommittee.

Eric earned his doctorate degree in teaching and curriculum from Syracuse University in 1993.

Jim Nance, EdS, is an associate professor of kinesiology and health promotion at the University of Kentucky, Lexington. He has more than 30 years of experience teaching college physical education majors how to teach gymnastics. He also coached gymnastics for 9 years and judged for 20 years. For 17 years he directed the Kentucky High School Gymnastics Championships.

Jim is a member of the USA Gymnastics Education Subcommittee and a life member of AAHPERD. He has received several service awards for his gymnastics clinics and workshops, including the USA Gymnastics Service Award in 1991 and the University of Kentucky Achievement in Service Award in 1985 and 1992. Jim earned his EdS degree from Eastern Kentucky University in 1979.

Patty, Eric, and Jim are also coauthors of three other books: *Sequential Gymnastics II* (which is used by USA Gymnastics as part of its certification program), *I Can Do Gymnastics Beginner*, and *I Can Do Gymnastics Intermediate*. Like *Gymnastics Fun and Games*, these books were also designed for use in a school setting.